The Little Book of
～ HOME ～
PRESERVING

By Rebecca Gagnon

P PETER PAUPER PRESS, INC.
WHITE PLAINS, NEW YORK

For my mom who always worked to make us great food, my dad who taught us how to appreciate growing it, and my husband who understands my need to create in the kitchen

Text and photographs copyright © 2013 by Rebecca Gagnon
The following photos are courtesy of Shutterstock Images:
Cover: © Markus Mainka; pp. 1, 173: © Nattika; p. 4: © fotogiunta;
p. 6: © teleginatania; p. 9: © Ivan Polishchyk; p. 13: © librakv; p. 31:
© Brent Hofacker; p. 44: © Dmitry_Tsvetkov; p. 49: © Candace
Hartley; p. 51: © Roxana Bashyrova; p. 55: © gaborcsordas; p. 59:
© Dionisvera; p. 83: © catlook; p. 96: © Lesya Dolyuk; p. 99:
© Dream79; p. 100: © Glenn Price; p. 108: © Wiktory; p. 145:
© Teri Virbickis; p. 146: © sarsmis; p. 170: © Ian 2010

The Little Book of
ᜍᜎᜈ HOME ᜍᜎᜈ
PRESERVING

TABLE of CONTENTS

INTRODUCTION

Not that long ago, if you wanted strawberries in January, you had to make sure you saved some from your own growing season—by canning, freezing, or dehydrating them until you were ready to eat them. Modern advances in the way we grow, handle, and transport our food may mean that we are no longer bound by the hard and fast rules of seasonality, but a return to old-fashioned, in-season, slow food is certainly on the rise. Even though we now have the option of frozen and industrially canned foods lining the shelves at the supermarket, these conveniences may not live up to our taste standards, or our deepening commitments to purchase foods locally and sustainably grown.

Preserving foods yourself is empowering, and transports you back to the very moment of a food's peak vibrancy. It is generally a more wholesome, economic, and ecological food choice as well, since buying locally at the peak of the season, taking care to choose it yourself, and using sound methods to store safely in jars, uses less resources than the alternative. More than simply participating in a fad, it is a lifestyle choice, one that can often result in doing more for yourself, your family, and others—and in being less reliant on a food system that seems hopelessly flawed at times. It is an exercise in good taste and preparedness, and is a good skill to pass on.

I grew up in rural, northern Wisconsin, where the local grocery prices were driven in part by the year-round tourism industry that surrounded our picturesque lakes, trails, and campgrounds and in part by the transportation costs to get products far north. My family was close-knit; we all gardened and shared in producing and preserving foods to sustain us through what seemed, at times, like endless winters. As a child I learned the importance of both growing and preserving food, though it wasn't until I had a child of my own that I began to develop my own skill of preserving. Because I grew up in a family of gardeners, I felt that I needed to grow what I wanted to put in jars. But realizing that I could take a few pounds of fruits and vegetables that I didn't grow myself and preserve them was a revelation! It freed me from thinking that I had to do everything myself. I discovered that excellent results could come from subtropical supermarket mangoes just as well as anything that I grew in my own garden.

Preserving at home doesn't always have to mean canning in a hot water bath or pressure cooker. It can be as simple as letting some fruit relax in alcohol, or letting cabbage ferment naturally with the aid of some salt. In this book, I will focus mainly on hot water bath canning, easy preservation by using alcohol or vinegar, and another unique natural preservation method called lacto-fermentation. All of these methods do not require much in the way of specialty equipment, and in fact you may be able to use kitchen items you already have on hand.

PRESERVING BASICS

SAFETY

Whenever the subject of hot water bath canning comes up, so do the horror stories of those poor souls who attempted to preserve low-acid foods in the wrong way . . . resulting in death. It's unfortunate that this prevents many people from learning the art of canning! Once you know what is safe to can, and what parts of the canning process are customizable to your taste (and which are not), you are enlightened with a whole new world of food possibilities.

So what exactly is safe to can in a hot water bath? Basically anything high in acid is perfectly fine for this method. The most common high-acid fruits are apples, cranberries, rhubarb, and citrus fruits, and low-acid fruits can easily have acid added, to make them safe for hot water bath canning. *Clostridium botulinum* (a toxic bacteria that can grow in air-tight, low-acid environments leading to botulism) is the chief worry of home canned food, and it simply can't grow where the acid is lower than a pH of 4.6. If you stick to reputably-published recipes and follow good canning procedures, home canning is a safe and rewarding way to preserve food.

There are several sites online that can answer questions pertaining to home preservation. One of the best is the

National Center for Home Food Preservation *(http://nchfp.uga.edu/)*, which includes information from the USDA on safe procedures and recipes, and a listing of the Cooperative Extension System. The Extension System is organized by state and is an invaluable tool that allows you to directly communicate with master preservers in your area of the United States. You can ask specific questions about safety of recipes or procedures. The information your local Extension office provides is also the most current advice available on a particular topic.

As armed with knowledge as you can be when starting a journey in home canning, using common sense is probably the best advice anyone could ever give you. If you take a jar off the shelf several months after canning and the seal has broken, it has developed mold, or smells strange, looks strange, or just gives you a strange feeling: toss the contents out. It is always better to be safe rather than sorry.

INGREDIENTS

Choosing the ingredients for home preservation is perhaps the most important part of the process. **Fruits and vegetables** should be at their peak of freshness and not close to spoilage—ideally they should also be home-grown, locally grown, or organically grown. In particular, I am finicky about using organic citrus in my personal canning. I do not live in a citrus-growing region, and organic citrus comes with the guarantee that the fruits are not waxed or sprayed with artificial colors: important things to consider since I adore using their zests to flavor jams, jellies, and preserves.

Of course, sometimes using **frozen fruit** yields excellent results as well. I often freeze various berries and rhubarb to make into jams at later dates. They always keep their integrity, and the end result is often as good as if you made them with fresh produce. I actually prefer to make my rhubarb jam "on demand" this way, rather than canning it for long-term storage (though rhubarb's high-acid content makes it perfectly suited to water bath canning).

Sugar plays a big role in sweet preserving, and I like to interchange raw sugar with granulated sugar. It weighs nearly the same, though I may use just a touch more of the raw sugar since the granules are larger and take up more room in the measuring cup. Substituting honey, agave syrup, or any number of artificial sweeteners for sugar is not recommended. If you are looking for recipes that use these types of sweeteners, look for a published recipe as a guideline and double-check with your Extension office.

Preserving jams, jellies, preserves, and conserves relies on the development of **pectin** in the fruit. Low-pectin fruits (watermelon, for example) may never develop a

gel without the aid of commercial (or homemade) pectin. In general I prefer the looser gel on natural pectin that develops with long cooking times, but occasionally I'll opt for the quicker gel made possible by a box of powdered or liquid pectin. Both types of pectin can usually be found in the sugar/flour/canning aisle of the regular grocery store, or wherever canning products are sold. Inserts included in the box will also give you basic canning information.

Vinegar or lemon juice is often called for in pickling recipes. Generally speaking, all vinegars are interchangeable provided they have at least 5% acidity (often labeled as 50-grain). Never reduce the amount of vinegar in a brine solution, since it may reduce the overall acidity in the finished product. Lemon (or lime) juice can be bottled or fresh. Where it is used only as a means to increase the finished acidity of the product (as in whole tomatoes), I prefer the convenience and standardization of bottled juice. But where the citrus plays more of a role in the flavor of a preserve, I prefer the fresh version.

For home canning of pickles, you will sometimes see the use of **canning salt** in recipes. Canning salt is an extra-fine milled salt that is free of anti-caking agents, which means that it will dissolve fully—avoiding a cloudy brine product. Do not substitute table salt or other natural salts without some research: other natural salts have larger crystals meaning that you need more to equal the same amount. Minerals in natural salts can also lead to harmless cloudiness in your brine. Canning salt is inexpensive, and a large box (found near the sugar/flour/canning items in the grocery store) will last you a long time.

For some lacto-fermented things, **whey** is a common addition. Whey is technically not necessary for lacto-ferment vegetables, since a bit of additional salt will keep the vegetables from spoilage until the beneficial lactic acid bacteria take over the preserving process. In lacto-fermented fruits, however, whey is necessary to "kick-start" the preservation. The type of whey used in lacto-fermenting is made from draining unsweetened yogurt (or other cultured milk product). This type of whey is different from powdered protein whey you may find in the health food store, or from the whey left over from heated cheese-making processes. Cultured milk whey is full of live probiotics, unlike the heat-treated powdered, or cheese by-product, whey. You can make your own whey by following the **Homemade Whey** recipe on the following page. It's impossible to calculate the exact yield, since all yogurts are different and have differing amounts of moisture depending on the milk used, but this recipe will yield more than enough whey needed for recipes in this book.

HOMEMADE WHEY

WHAT YOU WILL NEED:

Funnel
Filter, very fine—such as a paper coffee filter
Glass jar (1 pint jar will be plenty large enough)
½ cup unsweetened plain yogurt

INSTRUCTIONS:

1. Line the funnel with the filter and place over a glass jar.

2. Place the yogurt in the filter and let drain for at least 2 hours. You can also let it drain overnight in the refrigerator. (The longer you let it drain, the more whey will be released.)

3. The drained liquid is the whey. Measure the required amount per the recipe instructions. Store any unused whey in the refrigerator for up to one week. Discard the remaining thickened yogurt, or use it as you would Greek yogurt or sour cream.

Alcohol is perhaps one of the oldest forms of preservation. Ancients essentially discovered a way of fermenting bread into beer, and the two distinct processes of bread making and beer making remain impossibly similar.

Alcohol technically never goes bad, and so long as a fruit is fully submerged, it would probably last forever as well (however, alcohol-preserved fruit generally tastes best within the first several months). When choosing an alcohol to preserve with, I think it makes good sense not to use the most expensive bottle in the store, but not a bottle of super-cheap, poorly produced alcohol either. Aim for one in the middle of the road—if it tastes okay by itself, then what you make with it will improve vastly!

Water is frequently called for in canning. Sometimes it is used in brines for pickles or as a dilution element for thick sauces. Because I live in a city and use city water, I always insist on using filtered or spring water. This way, I am assured that I have water without contaminates or off-flavors. If you live in a rural area, or are certain of the quality and taste of your tap water, it is fine to use tap water when water is called for.

BASIC EQUIPMENT

Getting set for home canning is actually a pretty easy endeavor. Although you may be able to use some of the equipment you have in your kitchen already, a few select purchases can make the process of hot water bath canning much easier.

Absolutely essential is a **large pot** (or water bath canner) to be used as a hot water bath. Any large pot will do—so long as it holds at least seven jars, and is deep enough to cover the jars by one inch of water. If you invest in a stainless steel pot, you will have it for the rest of your life. An enameled steel pot may last several seasons before needing to be replaced (depending on how hard your water is). Most water bath canners are 8 to 10 quarts, and if you buy one designated as a canner, it will also come with a lifting rack that keeps the jars from sitting directly on the bottom of the pot. If you don't have a lifting rack, you can use old canning rings, or a small, round cooling rack to keep the jars off of the bottom of the pot.

Next, of course, are **canning jars**. The most common jars in the United States are Ball® and Kerr® jars, both made in the U.S. by Jarden Home Brands. When sold new, they come with both rings and lids. The rings are reusable, but the lids are single use only. You are usually able to buy replacement lids and rings at the same place you found the canning jars: at larger supermarkets, hardware stores, or online. You are also able to sometimes find canning jars at thrift shops, rummage sales, or in your grandmother's basement! Older jars are fine to use, provided they are free from chips or cracks and use a two-piece lid/ring seal.

There are other companies that produce canning jars of specialty sizes and shapes. Germany's Weck jars are becoming more popular lately because of their charming design, and reusable glass lids. They are more expensive, and require a slightly different processing method. The information is available where you purchase the jars, or on the Weck website *(www.weckjars. com)*. National kitchen supply stores also carry foreign canning jars such as the Italian-made Bormioli Rocco jars. These are commonly sold with the processing instructions inside the jars themselves.

For the recipes in this book, we've measured the approximate yields in standard jar sizes that we feel make the most sense for each specific recipe. For example, the Kumquat-Habanero Marmalade *(see page 37)*, yields about 4 half-pint jars, and the Pickled Beets *(see page 139)*, yields about 8 pint jars. We chose to measure the marmalade in half-pint jars because this is a pretty standard size for jams, jellies, and sweet preserves. Opening a whole pint of sweet marmalade would be a huge quantity—even for a large family. While pickled items, such as the beets, store longer once opened, and are therefore commonly canned in pint jars. If you're preparing a recipe with the intention of giving away gift jars, you may want to consider using smaller jars, like a 4-oz. size. Whatever size jars you ultimately decide to use, make sure to follow the instructions regarding leaving the proper amount of headspace. There needs to be enough room at the top of the jars to ensure that there's room for the expansion of the preserves, while also making sure that there's not too much space, which can result in spoilage. Follow each recipe's specific instructions, and if you have leftover food that does not fit into a jar, store it in your refrigerator for immediate consumption (most things will last for about a couple weeks).

PINTS	OUNCES
Half-pint	*8 oz.*
Pint	*16 oz.*
Quart	*32 oz.*
Gallon	*128 oz.*

A **preserving pot** is needed to cook down sweet preserves and bring pickle brine up to a boil. Any non-reactive pot (which includes clay, enamel, glass, or stainless steel, but not cast-iron or aluminum) is fine, so long as it holds 6 to 8 quarts of liquid. I have an enameled steel Dutch oven that, at 5 ½ quarts, is sometimes a bit small but I make do, since it is my favorite pot and it conducts heat superbly.

Although the following items are not absolute essentials, they do make canning life more pleasant: a **funnel** (to help get food into the jars), a **jar lifter** (to add and remove filled canning jars to the water bath), and a **digital or analog thermometer**. Already most likely in your kitchen is a selection of **knives**, **cutting boards**, **basic measuring cups**, **spoons**, and a **ladle**. These can all be purchased in a good canning kit, as well.

A **kitchen scale** is not necessary, but is extremely helpful. Without a scale, you can have your produce weighed at your point of purchase, since most is purchased by the pound. In a pinch, a bathroom scale can weigh your homegrown produce. The recipes in this book use weight to measure the produce, so you will definitely need to make sure that you weigh your ingredients properly.

Sieves are also very useful for straining sauces. If canning large amounts of applesauce, for example, you might consider a chinois (China cap) strainer or a hand-cranked Foley food mill. They both do excellent jobs of removing cores and seeds from finished sauces. I inherited my grandmother's Victorio strainer, which is larger and more complicated to set up, but very efficient and can process a much larger quantity of sauce with the turn of the handle. If you become an avid canner, it is worth the cost, and pays for itself quickly with the amount of time it saves processing large quantities of fruit.

If you are a fan of crystal clear jellies, an inexpensive **jelly bag** for straining will help you avoid a cloudy jelly. Personally, I am not too concerned with the appearance of jelly, and I strain mine through a homemade bag made of unbleached muslin, which works just fine.

BASIC HOT WATER BATH CANNING METHOD

This basic method is used in most of the recipes in this book. You will need to refer to it often and become familiar with it. When you are reading a recipe and it instructs you to "ready the jars, lids, rings, and hot water bath" it is referring to steps 1 through 4. After you've finished preparing the food to be canned and are ready to fill the jars, refer to steps 5 through 10 (making note of each recipe's specified boiling process time). After a few canning experiences, you will find the basic hot water bath method easy to remember. You will also find your own rhythm that makes sense for the layout of your kitchen. (If you are using jars other than Ball® or Kerr®, make sure to refer to the jar's specific canning instructions, which are usually enclosed in the jar package at time of purchase.)

1. Wash canning jars in hot soapy water. Prepare an extra jar or two over the yield, in case you have more than you expect.

2. Sterilize the jars. (Some recipe books do not call for sterilization of the jars. The USDA recommends sterilization for all jams and jellies, and I sterilize most jars just to be on the safe side.) Sterilize the jars by submerging them in water in a large pot (or your water bath canner), bringing them up to a boil, and keeping them at a boil for 10 minutes.

After they boil for 10 minutes, then keep them warm until ready to fill. There's a couple different ways you can do this. You can keep them in the water (bringing it down to a simmer), until you are ready to fill them with food. At that time, remove them with a jar lifter and drain each jar individually and proceed with filling them. Or, I like to keep them in my oven, at 250°F. Just remove the jars from the water bath after boiling, and place them on a baking sheet and keep them in the oven until ready to be filled.

3. Prepare the rings and lids by placing them in a small saucepan with enough water to cover. Bring them to a bare simmer, cover the pan, turn off the heat, and let them sit until ready to use. Be careful not to boil the lids as it can cause the seals to break down.

4. Bring your water bath up to a boil (you'll have left-over water from the sterilization process, but you may need to add more to ensure that you'll have enough water to cover the jars by 1 to 2 inches). While the bath is coming up to a boil, prepare what you are canning. If the water comes up to a boil before you finish preparing the food, you can reduce the heat until your filled jars are nearly ready to go into the bath.

5. Set out the warm jars and fill them with the prepared food, most often leaving a headspace of ¼ inch unless otherwise specified in the recipe. Be sure to fill the jars to the proper headspace: too much space can cause a poor seal or spoilage, and too little may not allow for expansion of the preserve.

6. Use a lint-free cloth dipped in clean, hot water to wipe the top of the jar, and then apply the lid and the ring (see jar manufacturer's specific instructions for applying lids and rings). Tighten ring only to "fingertip tightness," which means do not tighten too much, but tighten enough to be snug. Air needs to be able to escape the inside of the jar.

7. Load the filled and covered jars upright into the water bath canner. If you have a canning rack, you can use it or simply load them using tongs or jar lifter one at a time.

8. Bring the water bath back up to a boil and process for the length of time as directed in the specific recipe. Begin timing your jars after a full, rolling boil has returned. The canner lid should be on during the boiling processing time.

9. After the boiling water bath process time is up, turn off the heat and remove the jars (with tongs or jar lifter) to a towel-lined countertop. Listen for the lids to "ping," which will happen as the jars begin

to cool and the seals are formed. Do not touch or disturb the jars until they are completely cool (12 to 24 hours).

10. Remove the rings from the jars, and check the seals. The lids should not buckle up and down, and you should be able to lift each jar carefully by its lid only. Store the jars in a cool dark place (without the rings on) for up to one year.

BASIC LACTO-FERMENTATION PRESERVATION METHOD

While hot water bath canning has a somewhat rigid set of rules, lacto-fermenting operates on a "wisdom of the ages" approach. It helps that if something goes wrong in the lacto-fermenting process, the resulting food will smell so bad that there is no way you would consider eating it. Lacto-fermentation is essentially a natural pickling process, most commonly applied to vegetables, however, some people enjoy fruit prepared this way as well. As vegetables break down, lactic acid bacteria grows, forming a natural preservative that keeps the vegetables safe to eat for many months under refrigeration. Most lacto-ferments have a particular sourness that is an acquired taste. Producing these healthful ferments at home is both easy and economical.

Lacto-fermenting also subscribes to the credo of "cleanliness not sterility." Because it is so closely related to the natural world, preserving this way actually incorporates the microscopic life that surrounds us, therefore absolute sterility is not necessary. Make sure that you preserve in freshly washed glass jars, and that the ferment is full to within 1 inch of the top. Seal the jars tightly, but leave a bit of wiggle room for overflow. Place the jars on a tray in case of spillage, (the bubbling of live cabbage in particular can make its way out of the jar).

Don't be afraid of leaving the jars at room temperature to ferment for a few days. The probiotic cultures grow best at a temperature of 70°F to 75°F. In cooler temperatures, it may take a few extra days. How can you tell if a ferment is ready? Taste it! If, for example, it still tastes like cabbage and not sauerkraut, you will need to wait a while longer. Like rising bread dough, it's impossible to calculate exactly how long it will take due to the changing environmental factors. With practice, your intuition will develop and you will know when it has fermented to its potential.

After the fermentation is complete, transfer jars to storage in the refrigerator. They will remain good to eat for several months. Discard if the contents of the jar smell or look bad, or if mold develops across the top. Properly preserved lacto-ferments will not have any of these problems.

THE ART OF JAM, JELLY, PRESERVES, AND CONSERVES

Most people know the difference between jam and jelly: jam is thicker and sometimes has seeds, and jelly is thinner and mostly clear. Preserves (a more old-fashioned term), refers to whole or sliced fruits that take up residence in a thickened syrup. The thickness depends on your cooking time, and they are lovely added to yogurt, or spooned on top of pound cakes and other foodstuffs that are empty canvases for delightful, preserved fruits. Conserves are related to preserves, but generally thicker, and sometimes with nuts. Nuts are a surprisingly good addition to home canned things—they can add a real touch of elegance.

Assessing when a jam is done can be an art—it takes skill, practice, and observation. There are several methods that are useful: carefully watching the temperature of the boiling jam, testing a teaspoonful on a chilled plate or spoon, and simply watching how the hot jam "sheets" off of a spoon held above the preserving pot. I like to keep several small white plates in the freezer for testing. When I feel the texture of the jam change as I stir, I test it on the plates by dropping a teaspoon of jam and then looking to see if I can draw my finger through it without the trail filling back in. I double check to see how close to 220°F the jam is on my candy thermometer. Sugar gels at 220°F, and that is enough to set most things. And finally I dip the spoon in the jam and hold it above the pot. Jam that has not yet set will drip off the spoon quickly, while gelled jam will form a tiny "sheet" at the edge of the spoon.

If something gels too much, you can slice it and serve it with a cheese plate, or thin it with water in a saucepan and make a sauce. If something doesn't set enough, you can "re-make" it by taking it out of the jars, returning it to the preserving pot, and returning it to a boil. (Even easier, you can just mix it with seltzer water and call it a soda mix!) With every attempt, you will learn something new. The important thing is that you don't give up and feel bad if things don't work out the way you thought.

A NOTE ABOUT THE RECIPES IN THIS BOOK

It is important to read all the way through a recipe before beginning. Many sweet preserves take some planning because the fruit may need time to macerate with sugar overnight in order to develop a deeper flavor.

Weight measurements are always more accurate than other types of measuring. While I find my home scale is in constant use, it may not be a good investment for you if you don't do a lot of cooking. Alternatively, you can use the scale at the grocery store, farmers' market, or weigh out homegrown produce on a bathroom scale.

Recipe yields can vary not only from batch to batch, but from season to season. This is most directly related to how much water the produce gets. It's important to be flexible and to also think ahead. I always prepare a few extra jars just in case I have more yield than is expected. Remember that if you don't quite have enough to fill a jar, you can still enjoy it now. Most things will fare just fine under refrigeration for at least a few weeks, especially if you pack it into a sterilized jar.

It's tempting to want to change a recipe to make it your own. You can do this within reason, and without altering the core amounts of acid, sugar, and produce. Nuanced flavor additives like spices and citrus peel are generally fine to add to a recipe, but refrain from adding extra low-acid vegetables (like onions or peppers), or from decreasing the amount of acid added to fruits. Lowering the acid can affect the safety of the finished product.

The USDA tells us that most home canned foods should be enjoyed within one year of their preservation date. It's a good idea to label your jars with a permanent marker just before transferring them to a cool, dark place for storage. Month and year is fine, but I like to include the day as well. It's a nice way for me to remember an exact point in recent history when I take a jar from the shelf!

The recipes in this book have been organized by season, but as mentioned earlier, feel free to use purchased produce—you may have a craving for strawberry jam in the winter! You don't have to feel restricted to use only seasonal items that you've grown yourself. A wonderful world of home preserving awaits you—all year-round!

SPRING RECIPES

CILANTRO-RAISIN CHUTNEY

YIELDS ABOUT 1 HALF-PINT JAR

Spring into this healthy chutney—which is unusual and yet very addicting. It may not be beautiful, but it is certainly beneficial because it is fermented with probiotic goodness, and delicious on just about anything. Try it on tacos, scrambled eggs, sandwiches, or on the side of a cheese plate.

INGREDIENTS

1 small bunch cilantro, stems trimmed

1 clove garlic, peeled and chopped

1½ cups raisins, soaked in warm water for 60 minutes

½ teaspoon fresh ground black pepper

1 teaspoon ground coriander

1 teaspoon ground cumin

½ teaspoon red chile flakes, or to taste

1 teaspoon fresh ginger, grated

1 teaspoon Kosher salt

2 tablespoons whey (see instructions on page 16)

Spring or filtered water, as needed

1. Sterilize the jar *(see page 22, step 2)*.

2. Pulse the cilantro and garlic in a food processor until coarsely chopped.

3. Drain the raisins and add them to the food processor, along with the black pepper, coriander, cumin, chile flakes, ginger, salt, and whey and pulse until well chopped and uniform in consistency.

4. With the motor running, add a little bit of water judiciously. Add enough so that the chutney isn't too wet, but nicely moistened. (If your raisins were fairly plump with water, you may not need to add any additional water.)

5. Pack tightly into the sterilized, glass jar to within ½ to 1 inch of the top, pressing down on the chutney so that there are no air pockets. Tightly seal, and let sit at room temperature for 48 hours before transferring to the refrigerator for cold storage. Well-fermented, this chutney will last at least 6 months in the refrigerator, but you will likely eat it up long before then!

KUMQUAT-HABANERO MARMALADE

YIELDS ABOUT 4 HALF-PINT JARS

I love the flavor of raw sugar in this marmalade, but substituting white granulated sugar is also fine. Don't be afraid of the blindingly hot habanero either: it only lends a warm undertone to this sunny marmalade.

INGREDIENTS

12 ounces kumquats, sliced thinly into small rounds (seeds removed and saved)

½ of a habanero pepper, stemmed and seeded (include the seeds for spicier marmalade)

5 cups spring or filtered water

4 cups raw sugar

1. Place the kumquat seeds into a spice bag, or tie them up into a small piece of cheesecloth and put them into a preserving pot along with the kumquat slices, the habanero pepper, and water. Bring to a boil, and boil uncovered for 15 minutes, skimming off any foam that may form. Remove the pot from the heat and cover with a towel. Let it stand at room temperature for 8 to 12 hours.

2. Remove the habanero pepper from the pot, (but leave the bag of seeds in). Add the sugar to the pot and place over medium heat, stirring until sugar dissolves. Increase the heat to medium-high and bring to a boil. Boil for 1 minute, and then remove the pot from the heat. Cover the pot again with the cloth, and let sit at room temperature for another 8 to 12 hours.

3. Ready the jars, lids, rings, and hot water bath *(see page 22)*.

4. Place the kumquat mixture over medium heat and bring up to a boil slowly. Then raise the heat and continue boiling until it passes the spoon test, gels when dropped on a chilled plate, or until the mixture heats to at least 220°F *(see page 27)*.

5. Remove the pot from the heat and remove the bag of seeds. Make sure to skim off any remaining foam. Let the mixture rest for 5 minutes.

6. Set out the warm jars *(see page 24)*, and ladle the marmalade into the jars to within ¼-inch of the tops.

7. Apply the lids and rings, and process in a hot water bath for 10 minutes *(see page 24)*.

MANGO JAM WITH CAYENNE AND BLACK PEPPER

Yields about 4 half-pint jars

In spring, mangoes start appearing very reasonably priced in some supermarkets. This recipe is just the thing to use those store-bought mangoes in, since not all of us can live in the tropics!

INGREDIENTS

1 lime, zest and juice

1 to 2 oranges, juice only

2 pounds mangoes, peeled and diced

2 cayenne peppers, stemmed, seeded, and roughly chopped (for a spicier jam, include the seeds)

3 cups raw sugar

Coarsely ground black pepper, to taste

1. Ready the jars, lids, rings, and hot water bath *(see page 22)*.

2. Zest the lime and put the zest aside. Then juice the lime into a liquid measuring cup.

3. Juice the orange(s) and add to the lime juice until you have enough juice to equal a ½ cup total.

4. Combine the mangoes, cayenne peppers, lime juice, and orange juice in a preserving pot and cook gently

over medium-low heat until the mangoes soften and are tender (about 15 minutes).

5. After the mangoes have softened, mash lightly with a wooden spoon, and then stir in the sugar and lime zest. (Taste a bit of the jam and if it isn't hot enough for you, add more cayenne pepper or a pinch of powdered cayenne pepper.)

6. Increase the heat to medium, stirring frequently to make sure all the sugar has dissolved. When the sugar has completely dissolved, raise the heat to medium-high, and add several grinds of coarse black pepper. Boil until a spoonful of jam mounds up when placed on a chilled plate.

7. Set out the warm jars *(see page 24)*, and ladle the jam into the jars to within ¼-inch of the tops.

8. Apply the lids and rings, and process in a hot water bath for 10 minutes *(see page 24)*.

GINGERED RHUBARB JAM

Yields about 2 half-pint jars, and 1 4-oz. jar

Ginger and rhubarb are natural partners, and this jam is great on toast, muffins, and any morning-time baked goods. I also like to make this jam in the winter using frozen rhubarb, since rhubarb freezes beautifully. I prepare premeasured gallon bags packed with already-chopped stalks, making this quick recipe even quicker. And if you have a little run-over jam that doesn't fill a jar, consider yourself lucky—you have some that you can eat right away!

INGREDIENTS

1 pound and 2 ounces rhubarb (fresh or frozen),
   roughly chopped

2 tablespoons lemon juice

1 orange, zest only

½ cup coarsely chopped crystallized ginger

1½ cups raw sugar

1. Ready the jars, lids, rings, and hot water bath (see page 22).

2. Combine all of the ingredients in a preserving pot.

3. Cook and stir constantly over medium-high heat until the jam "gels" (about 10 minutes).

4. Set out the warm jars *(see page 24)*, and ladle the jam into the jars to within a ¼-inch of the tops.

5. Apply the lids and rings, and process in a hot water bath for 10 minutes *(see page 24)*.

RHUBARB JUICE

YIELDS ABOUT 4 QUART JARS

There is something so satisfying about having your own juice on the shelf to enjoy over ice when rhubarb season is over. You can add a few strawberries or raspberries for color (and a little boost of extra flavor) if you like—just be sure to taste and adjust the sugar to your liking. This juice is excellent by itself, mixed with club soda, or as a cocktail component.

INGREDIENTS

3 pounds rhubarb, roughly chopped

3 quarts spring or filtered water

2¼ cups granulated sugar

1 to 2 cups raspberries or strawberries* (optional)

1. Ready the jars, lids, rings, and hot water bath *(see page 22)*.

2. Place the chopped rhubarb into a preserving pot and cover with the water. Bring to a simmer over medium-high heat, and cook until the rhubarb is tender and almost mushy (about 20 minutes).

3. Add the sugar and berries (if using), and continue to cook, stirring frequently, until the sugar is fully dissolved.

4. Strain the liquid through cheesecloth or a fine mesh sieve into a bowl, and then return the liquid to the pot and simmer over medium heat for about 3 minutes.

5. Set out the warm jars *(see page 24)*, and ladle the hot juice into the jars to within ¼-inch of the tops.

6. Apply the lids and rings, and process in a hot water bath for 15 minutes *(see page 24)*. Before removing the jars from the hot water bath *(per the instructions on page 24, step 9)*, first remove the hot water bath from the heat and let the jars stand in the hot water for 5 minutes. Then remove them to a towel-lined countertop to cool completely. This will help prevent the juice from seeping out of the jar as it cools, which can sometimes happen if the jars go from boiling to room temperature too quickly.

If using strawberries, cut them in half.

SUMMER RECIPES

AMISH PEPPER BUTTER

YIELDS ABOUT 3 PINT JARS

This authentic Amish recipe comes from my parents' neighbor, Lizzy. My mom was even invited into an Amish kitchen to learn how to make this deliciously versatile condiment firsthand! Hungarian hot peppers are long, thin peppers which come in a variety of colors (red, orange, yellow, and light green)—get them all for a more colorful butter. This recipe is scrumptious with just about everything: spread on a sandwich or crackers, as a dip for chips, and even eaten plain on a spoon!

INGREDIENTS

10 Hungarian hot peppers, stemmed and seeded (include some, or all of the seeds for a spicier butter)*

1 cup prepared yellow mustard

1 cup apple cider vinegar

1¼ cups granulated sugar

1⅛ teaspoons canning salt

¼ cup all-purpose flour

¼ cup, plus 2 tablespoons spring or filtered water

1. Ready the jars, lids, rings, and hot water bath *(see page 22)*.

2. The Amish use no electricity, so they grind the peppers in a meat grinder. If you happen to have a meat

grinder, go ahead and use it to grind the peppers. Otherwise use a food processor to chop them finely, or chop them by hand. (If chopping by hand, you may want to wear gloves to protect your skin from the heat of the peppers.) Put the chopped peppers into a preserving pot.

3. Add the yellow mustard, apple cider vinegar, sugar, and salt to the ground peppers and stir to combine well. Bring to a boil over medium-high heat, stirring occasionally.

4. Meanwhile, in a separate small bowl combine the flour and water to make a paste.

5. Once the pepper mixture has come to a full boil, add about half of the flour and water paste, stirring as you add it. Return the pot to a boil, stirring constantly to avoid lumps. If it feels thick enough (it should resemble a thick barbecue sauce or ketchup), do not add more of the flour and water paste. If it feels a little thin, add a little more of the paste and bring it back up to a boil. Continue to boil hard for 5 minutes. (Keep in mind that the pepper butter will thicken slightly as it cools.)

6. Set out the warm jars *(see page 24)*, and ladle the butter into the jars to within ¼-inch of the tops.

7. Apply the lids and rings, and process in a hot water bath for 10 minutes *(see page 24)*.

*Hungarian hot peppers can often be found mid-summer at a farmers' market. They are also sometimes called "sharps" or "half-sharps."

BACHELOR'S JAM (RUMTOPF)

YIELD DEPENDS ON YOUR CHOICE OF FRUITS!

Bachelor's Jam (also called Rumtopf) is a traditional tipple that practically makes itself. Layer fruits with sugar as they come into season. Never stir it, and rest it in a cool, dark place until nearly Christmas before stirring it only once and then decanting. Each year, you will be rewarded with a slightly different flavor depending on your ingredient choices.

INGREDIENTS

1 pound each of various fruits, at the peak of their seasons (good choices are strawberries, blueberries, blackberries, raspberries, peaches, plums, sweet or tart cherries, and apricots)
Granulated sugar, 1 cup for every pound of fruit used
1 large bottle (1.75 liters) brandy or rum*

1. Choose a large, non-reactive jar, crock, or pot to house your liqueur. I like to use a 1-gallon, glass storage jar that has a glass lid. (Put a protective layer of plastic wrap on top of the jar before topping with the lid, to act as a double barrier to keep pesky fruit flies away.)

2. Beginning with the first ripe fruits of the season (usually strawberries in late May or early June), add

one pound of sliced fruit to the pot. (When adding stone fruits, you can either leave the stones in, or pit them. It's also your choice if you would like to peel the fruits as well. I do not.)

3. Top the sliced fruit with one cup of sugar. Do not stir.

4. Top the sugar with a layer of alcohol—use enough to cover the fruit by at least 1 inch. Cover and repeat with the next addition of fruit when the time comes.

5. That's it! Now just be patient as the season progresses, adding fruit, sugar, and alcohol as you see fit until the pot is full. Should you be shy on a whole pound of fruit, adjust the sugar to compensate: ½ cup for a half pound of fruit and ¼ cup for a quarter pound. After the last addition, let the pot rest undisturbed for 2 months.

6. Decant the Bachelor's Jam into clean bottles (I like the swing-top variety), or get fancy and decorate an old liquor bottle. I like to house the liquid separate of the fruit, but it is fine to store the fruit in the alcohol and enjoy both together as a topping for bread pudding, ice cream, or pound cake. If you store the fruit separately, be sure to include enough of the infused alcohol to keep the fruit fully-submerged. The finished "jam" tastes best within a

few months, but will remain usable for at least two years.

A good-quality brandy or rum is preferable, but top shelf isn't necessary. Gin or vodka can also be used, but I think the sweetness of brandy or rum makes for a more complex end result.

BLACKBERRY PUNK JAM

YIELDS ABOUT 3 HALF-PINT JARS

Nothing seems more punky to me than adding booze to something, and that's just what I did when making this jam for a roundup on the popular DIY foods website Punk Domestics. I felt I had extra punk points by making my own orange liqueur, but feel free to substitute some from the store.

INGREDIENTS

2 pounds and 5 ounces blackberries

1 orange, zest only

3 cups raw sugar

2 tablespoons lemon juice

¼ cup orange liqueur (see page 160 for recipe)

1. In a preserving pot, mash the blackberries, orange zest, and sugar. Cover and let it macerate for several hours at room temperature.

2. Ready the jars, lids, rings, and hot water bath *(see page 22)*.

3. Decide if you would like seeded, seedless, or half-seeded jam. If your preference is seeded or half-seeded, sieve half or all of the jam through a food mill or china cap into a separate bowl. Then return the contents of the bowl to the preserving pot.

4. Add the lemon juice to the pot and heat the black-berry mixture over medium-high heat until boiling. Skim off the foam carefully, and continue to stir frequently until the jam starts to thicken and it passes the spoon test, or gels when dropped on a chilled plate *(see page 27)*.

5. Remove the pot from the heat and stir in the orange liqueur.

6. Set out the warm jars *(see page 24)*, and ladle the jam into the jars to within ¼-inch of the tops.

7. Apply the lids and rings, and process in a hot water bath for 10 minutes *(see page 24)*.

BLUEBERRY MIXED-CITRUS PRESERVES

YIELDS ABOUT 7 HALF-PINT JARS

This recipe tastes best with freshly juiced citrus. I also like to include the zests of each fruit to punch up the flavor, but you may omit them if you would prefer a more subtle citrus undertone. But don't omit the lime zest: blueberries and limes are such good friends.

INGREDIENTS

2¾ pounds blueberries
⅓ cup fresh orange juice (zest from 1 orange, optional)
⅓ cup fresh lemon juice (zest from 1 lemon, optional)
2 small limes, zest and juice
1 cinnamon stick, or ground cinnamon to your taste
6 cups granulated sugar

1. Combine all of the ingredients in a preserving pot. Over medium heat, stir until the sugar dissolves completely. Once the sugar is dissolved, increase the heat and bring the pot up to a boil. Continue to boil for 10 minutes, and then remove from the heat.

2. Cover the pot with a clean towel and let it rest overnight, or at least 8 hours, at room temperature (or in the refrigerator).

3. Ready the jars, lids, rings, and hot water bath *(see page 22)*.

4. Over medium-high heat, bring the pot up to a boil, stirring frequently. Continue to boil and stir until the syrup has thickened and a bit of the preserves mounds on a chilled spoon or plate *(see page 27)*. Remove the pot from the heat, and remove the cinnamon stick (if used).

5. Allow the preserves to rest for 5 minutes, stirring occasionally.

6. Set out the warm jars *(see page 24)*, and ladle the preserves into the jars to within ¼-inch of the tops.

7. Apply the lids and rings, and process in a hot water bath for 10 minutes *(see page 24)*.

CANDIED JALAPEÑOS

YIELDS ABOUT 7 PINT JARS

I had my first candied jalapeño years ago from a locally produced jar, and I knew immediately I had to figure out how to make them. Now I make many batches every summer—some to give away and some to enjoy myself. They can be used on practically everything—from tacos and nachos, to eggs and grilled cheese sandwiches. Their sweet-hot brine is an added bonus, too—add a bit to liven up potato salad or deviled eggs, or include some in your next Bloody Mary.

INGREDIENTS

2 cups apple cider vinegar

*6 cups granulated sugar (or use raw sugar instead—
it will make a darker syrup)*

*3 pounds firm, fresh jalapeño peppers, sliced about
⅛-inch thick (room temperature peppers are best)*

1. Ready the jars, lids, rings, and hot water bath *(see page 22)*.

2. In a preserving pot set over medium-high heat, bring the apple cider vinegar and sugar to a boil. Reduce heat and simmer for 5 minutes.

3. Add the jalapeño pepper slices to the pot. Turn up

the heat and bring the pot back up to a boil, and then reduce heat and simmer for 4 minutes.

4. Set out the warm jars *(see page 24)*, and use a slotted spoon to transfer the peppers into the jars to within ¼-inch of the tops. (Keep the remaining syrup in the pot.)

5. Heat the pot on medium-high heat, and bring the syrup up to a full rolling boil. Boil hard for 6 minutes. (The syrup should reach about 220°F.)

6. Ladle the boiling syrup into the jars over the jalapeño slices, distributing equally among the jars. Insert a chopstick (or a small icing spatula), into the bottom of the jar two or three times to release any trapped pockets of air. Adjust the level of the syrup if necessary, to keep the jars full to within ¼-inch from the tops.

7. Apply the lids and rings, and process in a hot water bath for 15 minutes *(see page 24)*.

Note: Don't forget that jalapeños pack some heat, so there are some precautionary measures you may want to consider. While slicing the jalapeños, you might want to wear plastic or rubber gloves—the heat can irritate your skin. Also make sure to work in a well-ventilated area when preparing this recipe.

CITRUS CHAI GROUND CHERRY PRESERVES

YIELDS ABOUT 2 HALF-PINT JARS, AND 1 4-OZ. JAR

Ground cherries are actually not cherries at all but instead, are related to tomatillos. They share the same earthy sourness as the tomatillo, but also have a pleasant sweetness that makes them perfect in this chai tea-infused preserve. Try it alongside some sharp English cheddar and you won't be sorry.

INGREDIENTS

1 pound and 9 ounces ground cherries

1 lemon, juice and half of its zest

1 orange, zest and juice

1 heaping tablespoon of chai tea leaves

¼ teaspoon ground ginger (omit if your chai tea has a lot of ginger in it)

2 cups granulated sugar

1. Combine all of the ingredients in a preserving pot and bring to a boil over medium-high heat. Stir to make sure the sugar dissolves and then remove the pot from the heat. Cover and let the pot sit at room temperature (or in the refrigerator) for 8 to16 hours.

2. Ready the jars, lids, rings, and hot water bath *(see page 22)*.

3. Over medium-high heat, bring the pot up to a rapid boil.* Stir constantly until desired consistency is reached, and the jam gels when placed on a chilled plate *(see page 27)*. Remove the pot from the heat.

4. Set out the warm jars *(see page 24)*, and ladle the preserves into the jars to within ¼-inch of the tops.

5. Apply the lids and rings, and process in a hot water bath for 10 minutes *(see page 24)*.

* You can choose to mash about half of the ground cherries with a potato masher when they are halfway to the gel point, or you can leave all the ground cherries whole if you prefer. Also, taste-test the jam as it boils—you may want to add another ¼ teaspoon ground ginger if it doesn't taste "gingery" enough!

ELDERBERRY DRINKING VINEGAR

YIELDS ABOUT 5 HALF-PINT JARS

I enjoy tart, healthy drinks (such as kombucha), so when I discovered that I could flavor raw cider vinegar with nearly any fruit or berry, I was pretty excited. Drinking vinegars are sweet and concentrated, and usually diluted with seltzer or still water, turning them into Prohibition-style "Shrub Cocktails". Elderberries are powerful antioxidants—real cold- and flu-fighters. I drink this in moderation if I feel an illness coming on, and I like to think it works to squelch it!

INGREDIENTS

2 pounds ripe elderberries

1 quart raw apple cider vinegar (such as Bragg's)

4 to 6 cups granulated sugar

1. Separate the tiny elderberries from their stems. (An easy way to do this is to place them in the freezer for a half hour, and then comb through them with a sterilized, wide-toothed comb.)

2. Place the elderberries in a large glass bowl, crush them gently with a masher, and cover them with the vinegar. Cover tightly with plastic wrap, and store

somewhere at room temperature out of direct sunlight for 1 week.

3. Strain the vinegar out of the elderberries into a large bowl, using a fine mesh sieve. Press gently on the berries to help them release all of their remaining juices. The vinegar will be a beautiful purple color.

4. Measure the vinegar and pour it into a preserving pot. For every 1 cup of vinegar, add ¾ to 1 cup of granulated sugar. Over very low heat, stir the vinegar until the sugar melts. (Keeping the vinegar well below the boiling point helps it remain "raw" and healthful.) Once the sugar is fully-dissolved, turn off the heat and remove the pot.

5. Sterilize the jars *(see page 22, step 2)*.

6. Let the drinking vinegar cool completely before storing in sterilized airtight glass bottles or canning jars at room temperature, where it will remain good for one year. To enjoy, pour 2 tablespoons in the bottom of a glass, and top with seltzer or still water.

ESCABECHE

YIELDS ABOUT 4 PINT JARS

In Mexican cooking, escabeche (a mixed vegetable pickle with a kick), is often served alongside fish or meat dishes. In my family, it's welcome beside almost any Mexican meal—and if you are short on time, half or quarter the recipe and simply pack into sterilized jars. Pop them in the refrigerator for a week to cure, and then enjoy within a month or so!

INGREDIENTS

For the vegetables:

2 pounds fresh jalapeños, sliced about ⅛-inch thick

2 carrots, peeled and sliced about ⅛-inch thick

2 onions, sliced about ⅛-inch thick

4 teaspoons Mexican oregano*

4 cloves of garlic, peeled and sliced in half

For the brine:

¾ cup extra virgin olive oil

¾ cup spring or filtered water

3 cups white vinegar

1 tablespoon canning salt

1. Ready the jars, lids, rings, and hot water bath *(see page 22)*.

2. Set out the warm jars and pack them with a mixture of the vegetables, putting 1 teaspoon of Mexican oregano and 1 clove of garlic in each. Make sure to get a variety of vegetables in each jar.

3. Combine all of the brine ingredients in a preserving pot and bring to a full rolling boil over medium-high heat.

4. Carefully ladle the brine into each of the jars to within ¼-inch of the tops.

5. Apply the lids and rings, and process in a hot water bath for 10 minutes *(see page 24)*.

You can find Mexican oregano in the Latin food aisle of your grocery store, or at an ethnic market.

GRAM'S DILL PICKLES

YIELDS ABOUT 8 PINT JARS

My mom tried out different dill pickle recipes for years before going back to my gram's tried-and-true recipe—so there was no question what recipe I would use when I started making dill pickles myself! This is a classic dill pickle, and so easy to make. I like to find small pickling cucumbers that don't need to be sliced—I feel they keep their crispness better that way—but you can slice the cucumbers in spears or chunks if you prefer.

INGREDIENTS

7½ cups spring or filtered water

3 cups white vinegar

½ cup canning or pickling salt

8 cloves of garlic, peeled and cut in half

8 dill stalks (one for each jar)

5 pounds small pickling cucumbers, scrubbed clean,
   blossom ends trimmed off

1. Ready the jars, lids, rings, and hot water bath *(see page 22)*.

2. Make the brine by combining the water, vinegar, and pickling salt in a preserving pot and bringing it to a boil. Once it boils, reduce the heat and keep it at a low simmer until ready to use.

3. Set out the warm jars *(see page 24)*, and pack each of the jars with 1 clove of garlic (sliced in half), and one stalk of dill. Then fill them with the cucumbers. Pack them tightly, but not so tightly that you damage them. I try to get most of the cucumbers to line up perpendicularly in the jar.

4. Carefully fill each jar with brine to within ½-inch of the top. Insert a chopstick (or a small icing spatula), into the bottom of the jar two or three times to release any trapped pockets of air. (You can also gently tap the jar on the counter to release air pockets.) Adjust the level of the brine if necessary, to keep the jars full to within ½-inch from the tops.

5. Apply the lids and rings, and process in a hot water bath for 5 minutes *(see page 24)*.

Note: Let the jars sit for a month before opening, to complete their pickling process. (I know that is hard, but try to let them sit for at least 2 weeks if you can't wait a whole month!)

LIMEY RUM SOUR CHERRY PRESERVES

YIELDS ABOUT 5 HALF-PINT JARS

I love the thick, syrupy consistency of preserves. These whole cherries feel luxurious, and look gorgeous on top of buttered toast, thick Greek yogurt, or decorating a simple slice of chocolate cake.

INGREDIENTS

2½ pounds sour cherries, pitted (any juices saved)
1 lime, zest and 2 tablespoons juice reserved
5 cups raw sugar
¼ cup dark, spiced rum

1. In a preserving pot combine the cherries, cherry juice, lime zest, and sugar. Cover the pot, and let it sit for at least 1 hour.

2. After an hour, the sugar will have drawn out some of the cherry juice. Heat the mixture over medium heat, stirring gently and occasionally, until the sugar dissolves completely. Raise the heat to medium-high, and boil for 5 minutes, stirring occasionally. Remove the pot from the heat, and cover with a cloth. Let the pot sit at room temperature (or in the refrigerator) for 8 to 12 hours.

3. Ready the jars, lids, rings, and hot water bath *(see page 22)*.

4. Set the pot over medium heat and stir in the lime juice. Increase the heat to medium-high and bring up to a boil, stirring often while skimming any foam. Continue boiling until the syrup thickens and gels when dropped on a chilled plate *(see page 27)*. It can take at least 35 minutes until the thickness is reached. Add the rum near the end of the boiling time, and continue to boil for 5 minutes after adding it.

5. Set out the warm jars *(see page 24)*, and ladle the preserves into the jars to within ¼-inch of the tops.

6. Apply the lids and rings, and process in a hot water bath for 10 minutes *(see page 24)*.

PEACHY BBQ SAUCE

YIELDS ABOUT 9 HALF-PINT JARS

This barbecue sauce is a welcome departure from traditional tomato-based sauce, but it's not so unusual that
the picky eaters in your bunch won't also enjoy it. Try
it on grilled pork (or tofu), or anywhere else you might
enjoy a tangy barbeque kick.

INGREDIENTS

4 pounds peaches

¼ cup fresh lemon juice (about 1 large lemon)

½ cup extra virgin olive oil

1 large sweet onion, medium chopped
   (about 8 ounces or 1 cup)

5 cloves garlic, finely chopped

1½ cups dark brown sugar, firmly packed

1 cup apple cider vinegar

½ cup spring or filtered water

¼ cup tomato paste

1 cup Worcestershire sauce

4 tablespoons grated fresh ginger

1 tablespoon red chile flakes, or more to taste

*1 to 2 teaspoons garlic powder (I like to use the garlic gran-
   ules that I find in the bulk spice section)*

2 to 3 tablespoons chili powder

1. Ready the jars, lids, rings, and hot water bath *(see page 22)*.

2. Prepare a pot and bowl for blanching and shocking* the peaches. First fill a large pot with water and bring to a rapid boil over medium-high heat. Separately, fill a large bowl with cold water and ice cubes and place it in a spot where you can easily transfer the peaches out of the boiling water and into the ice-cold water quickly.

3. Remove the skins from the peaches by blanching them, several at a time, in boiling water. Blanch them for about 1 minute. Then, using a slotted spoon, transfer the peaches to the ice-water bowl to cool for 1 minute. You should then be able to easily slip the skins off of the peaches by gently peeling them back with a knife. Then chop the peaches into medium-size chunks.

4. Place the chopped peaches and lemon juice in a large bowl and stir to combine.

5. In a preserving pot, heat the oil over medium heat. Add the onion and garlic, and sauté gently until tender (about 10 minutes).

6. Stir in the peach & lemon juice mixture, dark brown sugar, apple cider vinegar, and water. Bring up to a boil, then reduce the heat to low and continue to simmer until the peaches and onions are very soft (about a ½ hour).

7. If you have an immersion blender, use it in the pot to puree the peach mixture until smooth. Otherwise, cool the contents of the pot for several minutes, and in batches puree the mixture in a blender. When all of the sauce is blended thoroughly, return it to the preserving pot.

8. Add the tomato paste, Worcestershire sauce, ginger, chile flakes, garlic powder, and chili powder to the sauce. Stir well to combine and taste to adjust the seasoning.

9. Bring the pot up to a boil over medium heat, and then reduce the heat and simmer uncovered until hot throughout (about 10 minutes). (During the simmering, continue to stir frequently, and taste again to adjust the seasoning. I like BBQ sauce on the spicy side, so I often add more chile flakes!)

10. Set out the warm jars *(see page 24)*, and ladle the hot sauce into the jars to within ¼-inch of the tops.

11. Apply the lids and rings, and process in a hot water bath for 15 minutes *(see page 24)*.

"Blanching" refers to the technique of partially cooking items by briefly plunging them into rapidly boiling water. "Shocking" is the technique of plunging food into an ice-cold water bath, to quickly stop the cooking process.

PERSIMMON-VANILLA JAM

Yields about 7 half-pint jars

The unique texture of a ripe persimmon could be likened as a cross between a tomato and a peach or apricot, but the flavor is truly one of a kind. The astringent notes of the Hachiya persimmon (one of the most common supermarket varieties), hold up against the large amount of sugar in this traditional box-pectin jam, and make it a worthy, seasonal treat around the holiday season. Try it on Greek yogurt or spread some on a chocolate cupcake for a simple, satisfying dessert.

INGREDIENTS

2 pounds very ripe Hachiya persimmons*
1 vanilla bean
¾ cup spring or filtered water
½ teaspoon butter (salted or unsalted)
½ cup fresh lemon juice (about 4 lemons)
1 1.75-oz. box powdered pectin
6 cups granulated sugar

1. Ready the jars, lids, rings, and hot water bath *(see page 22)*.

2. Prepare the persimmons by pulling the calyxes from the tops. Cut the persimmons in quarters, and scrape the flesh gently from the peels with a sharp

knife. Put the flesh of the persimmons in a preserving pot. Dice the flesh, or mash it with a potato masher, until it is of a uniform consistency.

3. Split the vanilla bean lengthwise, and scrape the seeds from the pod. Add the seeds and the pod to the preserving pot, along with the water, butter, lemon juice, and powdered pectin. Stir well.

4. Measure the granulated sugar into a large bowl and set aside. Over medium-high heat, bring the preserving pot up to a rolling boil (a boil that cannot be stirred down), add the sugar all at once, and stir well.

5. Bring the pot back up to a rolling boil, and once boiling, continue to boil for exactly 4 minutes. Remove from the heat and remove the vanilla pod.

6. Set out the warm jars *(see page 24)*, and ladle the jam into the jars to within ¼-inch of the tops.

7. Apply the lids and rings, and process in a hot water bath for 10 minutes *(see page 24)*.

*Note: Astringent persimmons, like the Hachiya variety, are ripe when they are very soft and the calyx top can be easily pulled away from the berry. Keep them out on your countertop to ripen. If you buy all of your persimmons at once, they may ripen at different stages—in which case you can peel the ripened ones and store the flesh of the berries in the refrigerator where they will hold for 2 to 3 days. If

you think a longer time is needed to ripen the rest of the persimmons (on your countertop), then stash the ripened flesh in the freezer and defrost it at room temperature before beginning the recipe.

SOUR CHERRIES IN LIGHT SYRUP

YIELDS ABOUT 6 QUART JARS

I prefer to preserve sour cherries in light syrup, since they seem to retain a bit more of their tartness. They're great to use in a pie, and if you don't end up using the whole jar in a recipe, be sure to make use of the delicious cherry-flavored syrup. You can use it in a number of ways: combine it with maple syrup and use it as a pancake topping, mix it with seltzer for homemade soda, or use it as a cocktail component.

INGREDIENTS

1½ cups granulated sugar
6 cups spring or filtered water
7½ pounds tart cherries, stemmed and pitted

1. Ready the jars, lids, rings, and hot water bath *(see page 22)*.

2. Combine the sugar and water in a preserving pot and bring up to a boil over medium-high heat. Stir until the sugar is completely dissolved, then reduce the heat to low, and keep warm until needed.

3. Set out the warm jars *(see page 24)*, and first ladle ½ cup of the hot syrup into each of the jars. Next, fill each jar with cherries to within ½-inch of the

top. And lastly, top off each of the jars with enough syrup to come within ½-inch of the tops.

4. Apply the lids and rings, and process in a hot water bath for 25 minutes *(see page 24)*. Before removing the jars from the hot water bath *(per the instructions on page 24, step 9)*, first remove the hot water bath from the heat and let the jars stand in the hot water for 5 minutes. Then remove them to a towel-lined countertop to cool completely. This will help prevent the syrup from seeping out of the jars as they cool, which can sometimes happen if the jars go from boiling to room temperature too quickly.

STRAWBERRY BALSAMIC SAUCE

YIELDS ABOUT 2 PINT JARS

The balsamic vinegar cuts through a little of what would otherwise become cloying in this delicious strawberry sauce. It is a medium-thick sauce, perfect for decorating a plate holding a chocolate torte, along with fresh berries in shortcake, or topping the weekend waffle. (And don't worry about the addition of vinegar: it's subtle enough that even children will love it!)

INGREDIENTS

1½ pounds strawberries, hulled

4½ cups raw sugar

6 tablespoons balsamic vinegar, divided

½ teaspoon unsalted butter (optional)

1. Place the strawberries and sugar in a preserving pot and mash lightly to combine. Cover the pot with a lid, and let it sit at room temperature (or in the refrigerator), overnight.

2. Ready the jars, lids, rings, and hot water bath *(see page 22)*.

3. Uncover the pot and stir the strawberries well; the sugar should be mostly dissolved. Puree the strawberries in the pot using an immersion blender. (Or,

remove the berries and sugar to a regular blender, then puree, and return to the pot.)

4. Add 4 tablespoons of balsamic vinegar and the butter (if using) to the pot. Heat over medium-high heat until the sauce comes to a boil. Boil the sauce for 5 minutes, skimming off the foam that forms around the edges. (There will be quite a lot of the foam. Don't toss it—you can use it to flavor yogurt, seltzer water, or as an ice cream topping!)

5. After the 5 minutes of boiling, add the remaining 2 tablespoons of balsamic vinegar to the pot. Stir well to disperse into the sauce (the sauce shouldn't come down from a boil).

6. Set out the warm jars *(see page 24)*, and carefully ladle the boiling sauce into the jars to within ¼-inch of the tops.

7. Apply the lids and rings, and process in a hot water bath for 10 minutes *(see page 24)*.

STRAWBERRY GUAJILLO JAM WITH ORANGE

YIELDS ABOUT 6 HALF-PINT JARS

This was one of the first jams I ever made with chiles, and it is still one of my favorites. The jam is soft-set without commercial pectin, and the deep, earthy flavor of the guajillo chile really brings out the flavor of the strawberry. Simply omit the chiles if you would like a plain strawberry jam.

INGREDIENTS

3 pounds strawberries, hulled

1 medium orange, peel and juice

2 dried guajillo chiles,* stemmed and seeded (for a spicier jam, include the seeds)

4½ cups granulated sugar

1. Add the strawberries to a preserving pot.

2. Remove the peel of the orange with a peeler, slice into thin shreds, and add to the strawberries. Squeeze out the orange juice and add it to the pot.

3. Chop the guajillo chiles into small pieces and add to the pot. Then add the sugar and stir carefully to combine.

4. Cover the pot and let it sit at room temperature (or in the refrigerator), for 8 to 24 hours.

5. Ready the jars, lids, rings, and hot water bath *(see page 22)*.

6. Uncover the pot and heat over medium heat. Stir gently to fully dissolve the sugar.

7. Raise the heat, and continue cooking until the jam boils, stirring and using a masher to break up the fruit as desired. Skim off any foam that forms. Continue boiling until a drop of jam mounds slightly on a chilled plate, or until the hot jam "sheets" off of a spoon *(see page 27)*.

8. Set out the warm jars *(see page 24)*, and ladle the jam into the jars to within ¼-inch of the tops.

9. Apply the lids and rings, and process in a hot water bath for 10 minutes *(see page 24)*.

You can find guajillo chiles in the Latin food aisle of your grocery store, or at an ethnic market.

WATERMELON CAYENNE JELLY

YIELDS ABOUT 7 HALF-PINT JARS

More than any other jelly I've ever made, this one elicits excitement from all those who try it. It tastes deliciously warm and is excellent on heated scones or buttered toast. Like most other chile-infused preserves, I also love it with cheese. It is particularly scrumptious with cream cheese.

INGREDIENTS

5 cups granulated sugar

1 1.75-oz. box powdered pectin

6 cups of watermelon puree (about 1 medium watermelon)*

3 to 4 fresh or dried cayenne peppers, seeded and sliced thinly into rings (include the seeds for a spicier jelly)

6 tablespoons lemon juice

½ teaspoon unsalted butter (optional, but helps prevent foam)

1. Ready the jars, lids, rings, and hot water bath *(see page 22)*.

2. Place the sugar and powdered pectin in a large bowl. Stir well to combine thoroughly and set aside.

3. In a preserving pot, combine the watermelon puree,

sugar and pectin mixture, cayenne peppers, lemon juice, and butter (if using).

4. Over medium-high heat, bring the pot up to a boil, stirring regularly, until the jelly reaches 220°F (about 20 to 30 minutes), or mounds on a chilled plate *(see page 27)*. Then remove the pot from the heat.

5. Set out the warm jars *(see page 24)*, and ladle the jelly into the jars to within ¼-inch of the tops.

6. Apply the lids and rings, and process in a hot water bath for 10 minutes *(see page 24)*. Make sure to leave the jars undisturbed for at least 24 hours as they cool. Check the jars by carefully turning one of them on its side to see if it has gelled.**

To puree the watermelon, cut the melon into chunks and discard as many seeds as you can. In batches, puree the chunks gently in a blender (or by hand with a potato masher). Then pour the resulting liquid through a fine mesh sieve into a bowl. Measure out 6 cups of the liquid for the recipe. Any leftover puree can be mixed with club soda for a refreshing agua fresca!

** It can be tricky to get a good gel set on watermelon jelly, because every melon varies in moisture. It can take longer than 24 hours for the pectin to develop, which is why it's particularly helpful to use a thermometer with this recipe, to make sure that the jelly gets to 220°F.*

WHOLE TOMATOES
(RAW-PACKED)

YIELDS DEPENDENT ON SEASON
(1 BUSHEL CAN EQUAL ROUGHLY
14 TO 17 QUART JARS)

This traditional tomato application is my favorite use for plentiful, flavorful, end-of-summer tomatoes. Canning tomatoes whole is extremely versatile: you can crush them gently by hand and strain them from their liquid for tomato sauce (use the liquid as you would tomato juice), or you can use the whole quart in soups or chili recipes throughout the winter. If you do only one thing with tomatoes, do this! You'll never return to purchased tomato products.

INGREDIENTS

Tomatoes
Bottled lemon juice
Spring or filtered water

1. Ready the jars, lids, rings, and hot water bath *(see page 22)*.

2. Prepare a pot and bowl for blanching and shocking* the tomatoes (which you will do later in step 5). First fill a large pot with water and bring to a rapid boil over medium-high heat. Separately, fill a large

bowl with cold water and ice cubes and place it in a spot where you can easily transfer the tomatoes out of the boiling water and into the ice-cold water quickly.

3. Set out the warm jars *(see page 24)*, and add 2 tablespoons of lemon juice to each jar.

4. Boil a large kettle or pot of water and keep it simmering on the stove.

5. Remove the skins from the tomatoes by blanching them, several at a time, in boiling water. Blanch them for about 1 minute, until a knife piercing the skin causes the skin to break open. Then, using a slotted spoon, transfer the tomatoes to the ice-water bowl to cool for 1 minute. You should then be able to easily slip the skins off of the tomatoes by gently peeling them back with a knife.

6. As you blanch the tomatoes, pack them either whole, sliced in half, or in chunks (as you prefer), into the jars to within 1-inch of the tops. Keep blanching tomatoes and filling jars until you have enough to process the first batch—7 quart jars usually fit in a standard-sized hot water bath canner.

7. Add simmering water (from the kettle or pot), to fill the jars to within ½-inch of the tops. Use a knife or thin spatula to poke around the edges of the jar several times to release any trapped air bubbles.

8. Apply the lids and rings, and process in a hot water bath for 45 minutes** *(see page 24)*.

*"Blanching" refers to the technique of partially cooking items by briefly plunging them into rapidly boiling water. "Shocking" is the technique of plunging food into an ice-cold water bath, to quickly stop the cooking process.

**The long processing time necessary for hot water bath canning of tomatoes can be shortened dramatically by processing in a pressure canner instead. You can also choose to fill pint jars instead of quarts, adding 1 tablespoon of lemon juice to each jar and processing for 40 minutes instead of 45. I think you get "more bang for your buck" by canning quarts. You may also be able to find someone who has a pressure canner with whom you can trade canning with—I trade preserves and pickled things with my mom, who puts up my yearly stock of pressure canned tomatoes for me!

AUTUMN RECIPES

AUTUMN SPICE PEAR SAUCE

YIELD ABOUT 5 PINT JARS

While I like applesauce without much adornment, pear sauce has a pleasant grit that can stand up to a bit of heavy fall spicing. Ample cinnamon, allspice, and nutmeg make this sauce a perfect (and simple) dessert.

INGREDIENTS

6 pounds Bartlett pears

1 cinnamon stick

1 teaspoon ground cinnamon (optional)

1 teaspoon freshly grated nutmeg

½ teaspoon allspice

1½ teaspoons ground ginger

2 tablespoons dark brown sugar (optional)

¼ cup spring or filtered water

1. Ready the jars, lids, rings, and hot water bath *(see page 22)*.

2. Peel and core the pears, and then cut them into small chunks. (If you have a food mill or chinois, you don't need to bother peeling or coring first.)

3. Combine the pears with all of the spices and sugar (if using) in a preserving pot. Add the water to the pot (this will just help the pears to start steaming).

Cover the pot and cook over medium heat, stirring regularly, until the pears are completely soft (about 20 minutes).

4. Remove the pot from the heat. In small batches, run the pears and their juices through a food mill or chinois set over a large bowl (or several smaller bowls) to remove the cores, peels, and pulp. When all the sauce is run through, return it to the preserving pot. (You may need to rinse the pot if stubborn bits of pear stuck to the edges.)

5. Bring the pot of sauce up to a boil over medium heat, stirring frequently until thoroughly hot.

6. Set out the warm jars *(see page 24)*, and ladle the sauce into the jars to within ¼-inch of the tops.

7. Apply the lids and rings, and process in a hot water bath for 15 minutes *(see page 24)*.

CLASSIC APPLESAUCE

Yields about 8 pint jars

Nothing gives you more for your money than homemade applesauce. Often, a paper grocery sack of not-quite-perfect apples can be found at fall farmers' markets for next to nothing. Once stewed down with only a cinnamon stick, you will wonder how you ever spent hard-earned money on bland, jarred supermarket brands. I leave mine unsweetened so I can use it in baking as well as enjoying it topped with a touch of cinnamon sugar.

INGREDIENTS

12 pounds apples, mixed varieties if you like

1 to 2 cinnamon sticks

¼ cup spring or filtered water

1. Ready the jars, lids, rings, and hot water bath *(see page 22)*.

2. Peel and core the apples, and then cut them into medium chunks. (If you have a food mill or chinois, you don't need to bother peeling or coring first.)

3. Put the chopped apples into a preserving pot along with the cinnamon sticks. Add the water to the pot (this will just help the apples to start steaming).*

Cover the pot and cook over medium heat, stirring regularly, until the apples are completely soft (about 20 minutes).

4. Remove the pot from the heat. In small batches, run the apples and all of their juices through a food mill or chinois set over a large bowl (or several smaller bowls) to remove the cores, peels, and pulp. When all the sauce is run through, return it to the preserving pot. (You may need to rinse out the pot first. If you would like sweetened applesauce, you may add a bit of sugar to taste at this point.)

5. Bring the pot of sauce up to a boil over medium heat, stirring frequently until thoroughly hot.

6. Set out the warm jars *(see page 24)*, and ladle the sauce into the jars to within ¼-inch of the tops.

7. Apply the lids and rings, and process in a hot water bath for 15 minutes *(see page 24)*.

You may need to cook the apples down in batches. Adjust the water and cinnamon sticks accordingly.

CONCORD GRAPE JUICE

Yields about 1 quart jar

If you are lucky to have access to Concord grape vines in the fall, this juice is an easy, rather old-fashioned approach to canning juice. Some people prefer to can grape concentrate and dilute with water before serving, but if you have the shelf space, bringing up a quart jar and simply straining out the spent grapes is better in my opinion. This recipe is for one quart, but make as many quarts as you have grapes to accommodate!

INGREDIENTS

1 cup Concord grapes
4 cups spring or filtered water
½ cup granulated sugar

1. Ready the jar, lid, ring, and hot water bath *(see page 22)*.

2. Wash and stem the grapes, and set them aside.

3. In a large kettle or pot set over high heat, bring the water up to a boil.

4. Set out the warm jar *(see page 24)*, and add the grapes to the jar, followed by the sugar.

5. Carefully pour enough of the boiling water over the grapes and sugar to cover and fill to within ½-inch

of the top of the jar. (You may not need the full 4 cups of water to cover.) Give a quick stir with a chopstick or long knife to combine.

6. Apply the lid and ring, and process in a hot water bath for 20 minutes *(see page 24)*. Before removing the jar from the hot water bath *(per the instructions on page 24, step 9)*, first remove the hot water bath from the heat and let the jar stand in the hot water for 5 minutes. Then remove it to a towel-lined countertop to cool completely. This will help prevent the juice from seeping out of the jar as it cools, which can sometimes happen if the jar goes from boiling to room temperature too quickly.

Note: After canning, let the jar sit for about 1 month to cure before enjoying. The color will deepen and the flavor will improve over a bit of time.

CONCORD GRAPE AND ROSEMARY JELLY

YIELDS ABOUT 7 HALF-PINT JARS

I first tried the combination of Concord grapes and rosemary in a genius focaccia bread recipe my friend Deena came up with. I couldn't believe how much more "grapey" the grapes tasted! I loved it so much that I now crave rosemary whenever I taste autumn's benevolent Concord grapes. However, if you prefer a plain grape jelly you can simply omit the rosemary.

INGREDIENTS

4 cups Rosemary-Infused Concord Grape Concentrate (recipe to follow)

7 cups granulated sugar

1 3-oz. pouch liquid pectin

1. Ready the jars, lids, rings, and hot water bath *(see page 22)*.

2. Combine the grape concentrate and sugar into a preserving pot. Heat and stir over medium-high heat until the mixture comes to a rolling boil.

3. Add the liquid pectin to the pot, and return to a boil for exactly 1 minute. Remove from the heat, and skim off any foam that may have formed.

4. Set out the warm jars *(see page 24)*, and ladle the jelly into the jars to within ⅛-inch of the tops.

5. Apply the lids and rings, and process in a hot water bath for 5 minutes *(see page 24)*.

Rosemary-Infused Concord Grape Concentrate:

3 to 4 pounds Concord grapes
Spring or filtered water
3 to 4 large sprigs of rosemary, needles removed

1. Stem and wash the grapes and place them in a preserving pot over medium-high heat. Add enough water (about 2 cups) to the pot to get some steam going before the grapes begin to release their own juices.

2. After the pot starts to simmer, mash the grapes with a potato masher. Reduce the heat so that they are boiling gently. Cover and continue to cook until the grapes are completely soft (about 30 minutes).

3. Remove the pot from the heat and let cool slightly. Strain the grapes through a jelly bag or muslin cloth, set over a large bowl for 24 to 48 hours at room temperature or in the refrigerator. (For a completely clear concentrate, do not disturb the bag or press on it to remove extra juice.)

4. Discard the grapes and jelly bag (or muslin cloth). Add the rosemary needles to the bowl and stir into the grape concentrate. Let the rosemary steep for at least 24 hours (in the refrigerator) to infuse the concentrate. After steeping, strain out the needles. (You can refrigerate this concentrate for up to 3 or 4 days until you are ready to use.)

CORTIDO

YIELDS ABOUT 3 PINT JARS

This was the first lacto-ferment I ever made, and it's still one of my favorites. The tangy bite is perfect on top of just about any kind of taco or tostada. The Mexican oregano really makes this special—I wouldn't recommend substituting regular oregano.

INGREDIENTS

1 large cabbage, cored and shredded
4 small carrots, sliced into about ⅛-inch rounds
1 large onion, sliced thinly
1 tablespoon Mexican oregano*
½ teaspoon red chile flakes
1 tablespoon sea salt
½ to 1 hot wax pepper (or any hot pepper), sliced into
    about ⅛-inch rounds
1 large, red or green jalapeño, sliced into about ⅛-inch
    rounds
¼ cup whey (see instructions on page 16)**

1. Sterilize the jars (see page 22, step 2).

2. Combine all of the ingredients in a large bowl or food-grade bucket. Use a sturdy wooden spoon to chop and pound the mixture for about 10 minutes, until the liquid from the vegetables is released.

3. Pack firmly into sterilized glass jars, and press down tightly to release liquid so that it fully covers all of the vegetables. Leave about 1 inch of space on the top, and screw lids on tightly.

4. Let ferment at room temperature for 3 days, and then transfer to the refrigerator for longer storage.

You can find Mexican oregano in the Latin food aisle of your grocery store, or at an ethnic market.

**If you prefer not to use whey, use an additional 1 tablespoon of sea salt instead.*

CRANBERRY GINGER CONSERVE

YIELDS ABOUT 3 HALF-PINT JARS

This sweet-tart condiment is a perfect addition to the Thanksgiving table, and don't forget to try it on leftover turkey sandwiches, too. Even better than the unique flavor is the fact that you can make it up in advance of the big day, and send a special guest home with his or her very own jar.

INGREDIENTS

12 ounces cranberries, fresh or frozen (about 3 cups)

1 cinnamon stick

1 large onion, medium chopped (about 1 cup)

1¼ ounces crystallized ginger, cut into small cubes (about ¼ cup)

1 orange, zest and ¼ cup of the juice

1 cup red wine vinegar

1½ cup raw sugar

1 teaspoon brown mustard seed

¼ teaspoon cayenne pepper

½ teaspoon ground cinnamon

⅛ teaspoon allspice

½ cup toasted walnuts

1. Ready the jars, lids, rings, and hot water bath *(see page 22)*.

2. Combine the cranberries, cinnamon stick, onions, crystallized ginger, orange zest, orange juice, and red wine vinegar in a preserving pot over medium heat. Simmer and stir frequently, until the cranberries pop and start to soften (about 10 minutes).

3. Add the raw sugar, mustard seed, cayenne, ground cinnamon, and allspice to the pot. Continue to cook and stir until the conserve begins to thicken (about 10 minutes). (The cranberries will continue to set as they cool, so don't cook too long.) Add the walnuts to the pot, and cook 5 minutes more. Remove the pot from the heat.

4. Set out the warm jars *(see page 24)*, and ladle the conserve into the jars to within ½-inch of the tops.

5. Apply the lids and rings, and process in a hot water bath for 10 minutes *(see page 24)*.

FIGGY CONSERVE

YIELDS ABOUT 3 HALF-PINT JARS

This conserve is what resulted when I happened upon perfectly ripe mesh baskets of figs in the supermarket. Since I don't live in a fig-growing region, I was happy to make something so beautiful with store-bought fruit! It's glossy and elegant, and really highlights the unique flavor of the fig. It is the perfect addition to any cheese plate.

INGREDIENTS

1¾ pounds very ripe figs, stemmed and cut in half
2 cups granulated sugar
1 orange, juice and zest reserved
3 tablespoons bottled lemon juice
1-inch piece of fresh ginger, cut into 3 slices
½ cup toasted walnuts

1. Combine the figs, sugar, orange juice, lemon juice, and ginger in a preserving pot. Cover and let macerate at room temperature (or in the refrigerator) for 12 to 24 hours. Stir occasionally at your convenience.

2. Ready the jars, lids, rings, and hot water bath *(see page 22)*.

3. Place the pot over medium-high heat and bring it up to a boil. Continue boiling it down, stirring frequently, until the contents are just about to reach the 220°F mark (about 20 minutes). (Skim any foam as needed, and remove the ginger pieces if you wish.) Then stir in the reserved orange zest and the walnuts and continue to boil for 3 minutes. Remove from the heat.

4. Set out the warm jars *(see page 24)*, and ladle the conserve into the jars to within ¼-inch of the tops. Insert a chopstick (or small icing spatula) into the bottom of each of the jars two or three times to release any trapped pockets of air.

5. Apply the lids and rings, and process in a hot water bath for 15 minutes *(see page 24)*.

JICAMA APPLE CUMIN KRAUT

YIELDS ABOUT 5 HALF-PINT JARS

I first had a version of this kraut as a type of raw coleslaw, made by my friend Annie Wegner-LeFort. After I decided to ferment it, the flavor deepened and became more complex. I love the color of the green apple with the green cabbage, too. It's refreshing—both to eat and to look at!

INGREDIENTS

½ large green cabbage, cored

⅔ jicama (about the size of a softball), peeled with a
   paring knife or sturdy vegetable peeler

½ medium sweet onion, thinly sliced

1 large green apple, cored and thinly sliced

1½ teaspoons sea salt

½ lemon, juice only

2 tablespoons whey (see instructions on page 16)

2 teaspoons cumin powder, or more to taste

¼ to ½ teaspoon cayenne powder, or more to taste

Handful of fresh basil leaves, chopped

1. Sterilize the jars (see page 22, step 2).

2. Shred the cabbage and jicama using a food processor (with the shredding disc), or by hand with a

knife. (If doing this by hand, cut the jicama into thin strips, or use a box grater.)

3. Place the cabbage and jicama into a large bowl and add the onion and apple slices, salt, lemon juice, whey, cumin, and cayenne. Use a sturdy wooden spoon to chop and pound the mixture for about 10 minutes, until the liquid from the vegetables and fruit is released. Do not worry about breaking up the apples.

4. Add the basil leaves to the bowl and chop (again using the wooden spoon), for about 1 minute to disperse evenly. Taste and adjust the spices according to your preferences.

5. Pack the kraut into sterilized glass jars with very little headspace. Tightly seal the jars, and let them sit at room temperature to ferment for 3 days before transferring to the refrigerator for storage.

PEAR GINGER GINGER JAM

YIELDS ABOUT 6 HALF-PINT JARS

Sometimes I feel like I simply cannot get enough ginger into a jam. It seems to mellow as it ages. So, I set out to make the most ginger-packed pear jam that I could, and this was the result. It is definitely for those who love ginger, but not so spicy that it's unapproachable on your morning toast. This is a jam that I love to stir into plain yogurt.

INGREDIENTS

3 pounds pears, ripe and giving to pressure, cored and chopped into medium chunks (with skin on)

2 ounces fresh ginger, grated (about a 3- to 4-inch piece of ginger)

1 lemon, zest and juice

5 cups raw sugar

1 cinnamon stick, broken in half

3 ounces crystallized ginger, cut into small cubes

1 tablespoon vanilla extract, or vanilla bean paste

1. Combine the pears, fresh ginger, lemon zest and juice, sugar and cinnamon stick in a preserving pot. Cover and let sit at room temperature (or in the refrigerator), for 8 to 16 hours, stirring every few hours or when convenient.

2. Ready the jars, lids, rings, and hot water bath *(see page 22)*.

3. Add the crystallized ginger to the pot and place over medium-high heat. Bring the pot up to a boil. Boil the jam down until it reaches your preferred consistency, and the jam falls nicely from the spoon, or mounds in a chilled dish *(see page 27)*.

4. Remove the jam from the heat and stir in the vanilla. Remove the cinnamon stick.

5. Set out the warm jars *(see page 24)*, and ladle the jam into the jars to within ¼-inch of the tops.

6. Apply the lids and rings, and process in a hot water bath for 10 minutes *(see page 24)*.

PICKLED BEETS

YIELDS ABOUT 8 PINT JARS

A lot of my old family recipes for pickling simply have the proportions for the brine. I suspect this is because you can do the simple math and accommodate as much as you care to harvest. Generally, brines are so quick to make up that you can do so on the fly—just after you realize you have more vegetables to pickle than you thought. These pickled beets are lightly spiced and are a great addition to a leafy green salad (with classic blue cheese and walnuts) or a simple relish tray.

INGREDIENTS

7 pounds beets

2 cups granulated sugar

2 cups spring or filtered water

2 cups white vinegar

1 teaspoon ground cloves

1 teaspoon ground allspice

1 tablespoon cinnamon

1. Ready the jars, lids, rings, and hot water bath *(see page 22)*.

2. Prepare the beets by washing them well and trimming the tops off (leaving about 1 inch of the root and stem ends in place). Place them in a large pot

and cover them with water (you may need to do this in batches depending on your pot size). Bring them up to a boil, and then reduce to a simmer until the beets are partially cooked (about 15 minutes). (You don't want to cook them too much—you want a beet with a bit of bite!)

3. While the beets are simmering, make the brine by combining the remaining ingredients in a kettle or pot and heating to a simmer over medium-low heat. Keep hot until ready to use.

4. After the beets are done simmering, remove them to a sheet pan to cool slightly. Using a sharp paring knife, cut the top and bottom ends off and slip the skins from them. Rinse briefly under warm water to remove any stubborn bits of skin, and then cut them into 1-inch chunks.

5. Set out the warm jars *(see page 24)*, and pack the jars snugly with the beets to within 1-inch of the tops. (It doesn't have to be exactly 1 inch, since the brine will be covering all of the beets—it kind of depends on the size of the beets and how "creatively" you can get them in the jar!)

6. Carefully fill each jar with the brine to within ½-inch of the tops. Insert a chopstick (or a small icing spatula), into the bottom of the jar two or three times to release any trapped pockets of air. Adjust

the level of the brine if necessary, to keep the jars full to within ½-inch of the tops.

7. Apply the lids and rings, and process in a hot water bath for 30 minutes *(see page 24)*. Before removing the jars from the hot water bath *(per the instructions on page 24, step 9)*, first remove the hot water bath from the heat and let the jars stand in the hot water for 5 minutes. Then remove them to a towel-lined countertop to cool completely.

SPICED SLICED APPLES

Yields about 5 pint jars

These soft apple slices work wonderfully to flavor oatmeal, or to stuff homemade hand pies or empanadas. They also stand on their own as a simple dessert topped with barely sweetened whipped cream. If you have extra syrup left over, count yourself lucky and glaze some pork chops, thin with water and enjoy a hot cider, or add to coffee for a surprising treat!

INGREDIENTS

3 cups raw sugar

6 tablespoons lemon juice, bottled or fresh

6 pounds Braeburn apples, or any tart and
   firm apple variety

2 cups water

1 lemon, zest only

2 teaspoons cinnamon

½ teaspoon freshly grated nutmeg

⅛ teaspoon allspice

½ teaspoon ground ginger

1. Ready the jars, lids, rings, and hot water bath *(see page 22)*.

2. In a preserving pot, combine the sugar and lemon juice.

3. Peel, core, and cut the apples into about ½-inch slices. As you are slicing the apples, add them to the sugar and lemon mixture to coat, and toss occasionally to avoid browning.

4. Once all of the apples are added to the pot, add the water, lemon zest, cinnamon, nutmeg, allspice, and ginger. Stir very gently to combine without breaking up the apples.

5. Heat the apples over medium-high heat and bring them up to a boil. Continue boiling for 5 minutes, while stirring carefully to avoid breaking up the apple slices.

6. Set out the warm jars *(see page 24)*, and using a slotted spoon, transfer the apple slices into the jars to within ¼-inch of the tops. Fill all of the jars with the apple slices, and then go back and ladle the remaining syrup over the apples, distributing equally among the jars. While filling the jars with syrup, insert a chopstick (or small icing spatula) into the bottom of each of the jars two or three times to release any trapped pockets of air.

7. Apply the lids and rings, and process in a hot water bath for 20 minutes *(see page 24)*.

WINTER RECIPES

BRANDY CRANBERRY JAM

Yields about 4 half-pint jars,
and 1 4-oz. jar

Cranberries are naturally festive with their sweet-tart nature and vivid red color—and a hit of brandy makes them all the more jubilant. Try this jam rolled up in your favorite "cinnamon roll" recipe with some toasted walnuts for an unexpected brunch treat.

INGREDIENTS

1½ pounds cranberries, fresh or frozen
2 Braeburn apples, peeled, cored, and cut into small chunks
1 cinnamon stick
3 cups raw sugar
1 orange, zest only
1½ cups spring or filtered water
½ cup brandy

1. Ready the jars, lids, rings, and hot water bath *(see page 22)*.

2. Combine all of the ingredients, except the brandy, in a preserving pot. Heat over medium-low heat until the cranberries burst and the apples start to soften (about 10 minutes).

3. Increase the heat to medium-high and stir constantly until the cranberries are completely broken down and the jam has a homogenized look. The jam will be thickened considerably.

4. Stir in the brandy, and continue to cook for 5 minutes, stirring frequently. (If the jam begins to thicken too much, add more water—2 tablespoons at a time—to loosen it.)

5. Set out the warm jars *(see page 24)*, and ladle the jam into the jars to within ¼-inch of the tops.

6. Apply the lids and rings, and process in a hot water bath for 10 minutes *(see page 24)*.

CHIPOTLE MUSTARD

YIELDS ABOUT 2 HALF-PINT JARS

For being some of the smallest seeds on the planet, mustard seeds really pack a powerful punch. They are naturally full of preservation power, and when paired with vinegar, their staying power only increases. This spicy mustard is a perfect addition to southwest-inspired burgers or as a dip for pretzel sticks.

INGREDIENTS

½ cup yellow mustard seeds

¼ cup brown mustard seeds

1¼ cup apple cider vinegar

1 to 2 chipotle peppers (canned in adobo sauce)

1½ to 2 teaspoons salt, to taste

1. Combine the yellow and brown mustard seeds in a glass bowl, and cover them with the apple cider vinegar. Cover the bowl and let it sit at room temperature until the seeds have soaked up all of the vinegar (at least 4 hours).

2. Sterilize the jars (see page 22, step 2).

3. Transfer the soaked mustard seeds to a food processor or blender and add the remaining ingredients. Feel free to add more chipotle peppers (or even just some of the spicy adobo sauce that they're packed in), if

you want more kick to your mustard. Keep in mind that the flavor of the mustard will change slightly over the first few days. You may need to adjust the salt level later.

4. Process or blend until the mustard seeds are partially broken and the mixture is creamy and evenly blended. Pack into sterilized glass jars (they don't need to be packed all the way up to the top). Cover with the lids and rings, and store in the refrigerator where the mustard will remain fresh for at least 6 months.

GRAPEFRUIT JAM WITH VANILLA AND POPPY SEED

YIELDS ABOUT 3 HALF-PINT JARS, AND 1 4-OZ. JAR

This jam is twice-speckled: first by minuscule vanilla bean seeds, and second by slightly larger poppy seeds. It's a tart jam with a bit of crunch—perfect with a winter's breakfast. Feel free to omit the poppy seeds if you dislike them, but they do add a welcome bit of nuttiness.

INGREDIENTS

8 large grapefruits (about 4 pounds)
1 vanilla bean
2½ cups granulated sugar
1 tablespoon poppy seeds

1. Ready the jars, lids, rings, and hot water bath *(see page 22)*.

2. Peel the grapefruits using a sharp knife, and be sure to remove all of the pith as well.

3. Working over a preserving pot (in order to save all of the juices), "supreme" the grapefruits by cutting through the sections and separating them from the membranes. Let the grapefruit segments and the juices fall into the preserving pot. As you work, set

aside any seeds you find (they are pectin-rich), and tie them up in a small section of cheesecloth. When done, add the cheesecloth bag to the pot.

4. Cut the vanilla bean down the middle lengthwise and scrape all of the seeds from it. Add the vanilla bean seeds and the vanilla pod to the preserving pot along with the sugar. Stir to combine.

5. Over high heat, bring the mixture up to a boil. Stir constantly, and continue to boil until the jam is just about to reach the 220°F gel mark. Then stir in the poppy seeds and continue to boil for 1 minute longer, or until it reaches 220°F. Remove the preserving pot from the heat and discard the vanilla pod and cheesecloth bag.

6. Set out the warm jars *(see page 24)*, and ladle the jam into the jars to within ¼-inch of the tops.

7. Apply the lids and rings, and process in a hot water bath for 10 minutes *(see page 24)*.

LEMON-LIME JELLY

Yields about 4 half-pint jars

Without boxed pectin, this tart jelly is softly set and gorgeous in mid-winter. You can decide if you would like to add the strips of lime peel, or leave them out. This jelly can also double as the easiest tea-time confection ever, by simply using it to fill a pre-baked tart shell and then chilling it. Enjoy!

INGREDIENTS

1 pound lemons, thinly sliced (preferably organic)
6 cups spring or filtered water
1 to 2 limes, peel only (optional)
¾ cup fresh lemon juice (about 6 lemons)
¼ cup fresh lime juice (about 2 limes)
3 cups granulated sugar

1. Put the lemons into a preserving pot, and cover with the water. Bring the pot to a boil over high heat. Then lower the heat, and simmer the lemon slices (uncovered), for 30 minutes.

2. Over a large bowl, drain the lemons through a jelly bag or fine mesh strainer (without pressing on the lemon pulp) until it stops dripping (several hours or overnight).

3. Ready the jars, lids, rings, and hot water bath *(see page 22)*.

4. If you are using the lime peel, use a vegetable peeler to peel the lime—avoiding any of the white pith. Then slice the peels into very thin strips and set aside.

5. Measure the drained lemon liquid. You should have about 4 cups. Top off the measure with a little extra water if you are short. Return the liquid to the pre-serving pot, and stir in the fresh lemon and lime juice, lime peel (if using), and granulated sugar.

6. Bring to a boil over high heat. Continue to boil, stirring regularly, until the jelly reaches the gel point (220°F).

7. Set out the warm jars *(see page 24)*, and ladle the jelly into the jars to within ¼-inch of the tops.

8. Apply the lids and rings, and process in a hot water bath for 10 minutes *(see page 24)*.

ORANGE LIQUEUR

YIELDS ABOUT 5 HALF-PINT JARS

Cara Cara oranges are a tangy, red-fleshed variety with a specifically nuanced orange flavor that's hard to put your finger on. I can find them mid-winter in my food co-op, and look forward to it every year. Grain alcohol is potent, scary stuff, and relies on dilution to make it fit for consumption. The volatile strength of it is perfect for drawing out all of the orange flavor (and color) from the citrus!

INGREDIENTS

6 to 8 navel oranges, peels only
4 Cara Cara oranges, sliced and dehydrated*
1 750mL bottle Everclear, or other grain alcohol
Simple syrup (recipe to follow)

1. Peel the navel oranges, using a peeler, to create strips. Then cut the strips into ⅛-inch sticks.

2. Put the orange peel strips and the dehydrated orange slices into a half-gallon canning jar or other large glass jar, and cover with the grain alcohol. Put the jar in a cool dark place, shaking every few days for about a month, to infuse it.

3. When ready to bottle and dilute, strain out the oranges and save the remaining liquid. The peel will

be bleached and pale, and the infused alcohol will be bright orange.

4. Measure the amount of the infused grain alcohol and then prepare simple syrup following the instructions below:

Simple Syrup:

Spring or filtered water, 1½ times the measure of the infused alcohol

Granulated sugar, ½ the measure of the infused alcohol

Measure the amount of water and sugar that you will need. Using a scale is particularly helpful for this. For example, if the beginning measure of the infused alcohol is 870 ml then you will need 1305 ml water, and 435 ml sugar. Heat the spring water with the sugar in a saucepan over medium-low heat, just enough for the sugar to dissolve completely. Remove from heat and let it cool to room temperature.

5. Sterilize the jars *(see page 22, step 2)*.

6. Combine the infused grain alcohol with the simple syrup in a large bowl or pot.

7. Over a large bowl, strain it through several layers of fine mesh cheesecloth. You may wish to remove the little bits of orange oil that you will see floating on the top, but I prefer to leave it unfiltered and enjoy the bitter orange flavor it imparts.

8. Once strained, store it in sterilized glass jars or swing-top-type bottles. Store in a cool, dark place. It's usually best to use it within the first year.

If you have a dehydrator, then you can dehydrate the oranges yourself: cut them into about ⅛- to ¼-inch thick slices, arrange them in a single layer on a dehydrator rack, and dehydrate them for 18 to 24 hours (until brittle and crisp) at a temperature of 130°F. Otherwise, non-dehydrated oranges will work if desired, but use only the peel (as per the instructions for the navel oranges in step 1).

To make a simple but very nice orange cocktail: add 1 part orange liqueur (1 oz.) to an old-fashioned glass filled half-full with ice. Add 5 parts (5 oz.) Cava Brut (or any dry sparkling white wine). Garnish with an orange or lemon peel, or a little shaved orange or lemon zest over the top.

ORANGE JELLY WITH LIGHT CHAI FLAVORS

YIELDS ABOUT 4 HALF-PINT JARS, AND 1 4-OZ. JAR

I really enjoy the flavors of chai, but sometimes chai-flavored things can be overpowering. Not so with this delicately flavored orange jelly. There is enough spice to keep it interesting, but not so much that it overwhelms the gentle flavor of in-season winter oranges.

INGREDIENTS

2 cups freshly squeezed orange juice

¼ cup fresh lemon juice

¾ cup spring or filtered water

1 1.75-oz. box powdered pectin

3½ cups raw sugar

⅓ vanilla bean

3 green cardamom pods, crushed lightly

1-inch piece of fresh ginger, cut into 3 slices

6 black peppercorns

1. Ready the jars, lids, rings, and hot water bath *(see page 22)*.

2. Combine the orange juice, lemon juice, water, and pectin in a preserving pot and stir well to combine.

3. Measure the sugar into a separate bowl and set it aside.

4. Cut the vanilla bean down the middle lengthwise and scrape all of the seeds from it. Add the vanilla bean seeds and the vanilla pod to the preserving pot. Put the crushed cardamom, ginger, and peppercorns into a tea ball or tie them up in a piece of cheesecloth and add them to the preserving pot.

5. Bring the preserving pot up to a boil over high heat, stirring constantly. As soon as it reaches a rolling boil (one that cannot be stirred down), add the sugar all at once.

6. Stirring constantly, return the pot up to a rolling boil and then boil for exactly 1 minute. Remove the pot from the heat and skim any foam from the jelly. Remove the spices and the vanilla pod and discard.

7. Set out the warm jars *(see page 24)*, and ladle the jelly into the jars to within ¼-inch of the tops.

8. Apply the lids and rings, and process in a hot water bath for 5 minutes *(see page 24)*.

PRESERVED LEMONS

YIELDS 1 PINT JAR

Preserving lemons in salt is perhaps the easiest form of lacto-fermentation. It took me awhile to appreciate their unique flavor, but as a fan of North African cookery I persevered until I genuinely loved them. I think adding a touch of sugar to the jar helped me on my way. It is wonderful to use them to flavor chicken and lamb dishes, or sautéed dark, leafy greens.

INGREDIENTS
1 pound lemons (about 5 medium-sized), preferably organic (I prefer thin-skinned lemons)
Kosher salt (about 5 tablespoons)
Raw sugar (about 2 tablespoons)

1. Sterilize the jar (see page 22, step 2).

2. Slice a small amount off of both the blossom and stem ends of the lemons. Then slice (but not all the way) each lemon into quarters starting at the stem end without going all the way through the lemon. (Essentially, you are making a deep "X" in the fruit.)

3. Working over a cutting board, pry open the lemon gently and sprinkle 1 heaping tablespoon of Kosher salt into each. Work the salt in by rubbing the fruit gently back and forth on itself a few times; lemon

juice will start to flow from the lemon. (Use a bench scraper to help collect any stray juices and salt from the cutting board back into the jar.)

4. Begin to pack the lemons on their sides into the sterilized jar. (I do not like to use wide mouth jars, since the shoulders on the regular jars help to hold the lemons down.) After packing 2 lemons into the jar sprinkle 1 tablespoon of raw sugar into the jar and continue packing. Press firmly on the lemons so that lemon juice begins to fill the empty spaces around them. After packing in 2 more lemons, add another tablespoon of raw sugar to the jar. Add the last lemon and press firmly to help the lemons fit.

5. You may have to wait several minutes for the salt to help the lemons start releasing more of their juice, but the lemon juice should easily rise to cover the fruit in the jar. If it does not, you can add the juice of an additional lemon to cover. Cap the jar tightly with a clean lid and ring, and shake well to disperse the salt and sugar in the jar.

6. Let the jar sit at room temperature (not in direct sunlight) for 2 weeks before transferring to the refrigerator where they will keep indefinitely. (Traditional cultures often store the lemons at room temperature.) Give the jar a shake twice a day as you think of it during the 2 week fermenting period.

Note: Technically the lemons are ready to use after 2 weeks, though many think their flavor improves over time. To use preserved lemons, remove a quarter of the lemon, scrape out and discard the flesh, and use only the peel.

RASPBERRY SERRANO JAM

Yields about 3 half-pint jars

In the dark of winter, it's good to know that you can make wonderful jam with frozen berries. The unique flavor of a single serrano pepper adds depth to rich raspberries, which reads as warm on your tongue—not too spicy hot. You can, of course, omit the pepper for a plain raspberry jam . . . but it's nice to spice up your winter with a little bit of heat!

INGREDIENTS

1½ pounds frozen raspberries
2¼ cups raw sugar
1 serrano chile pepper, thinly sliced
2 tablespoons bottled lemon juice
½ teaspoon unsalted butter

1. Ready the jars, lids, rings, and hot water bath *(see page 22)*.

2. Put all of the ingredients into a preserving pot. Bring up to a boil over medium-high heat. (If you have a spatter screen, it is useful to use it with raspberry jam; it is notorious for splattering.)

3. Boil the jam, stirring constantly, until you can feel it noticeably thicken. For most jams, you want to reach the 220°F gel mark, but in this recipe, that

can tend to "over-jam" these delicate raspberries. So in this case, aim for about 115°F to ensure a softer set.

4. Set out the warm jars *(see page 24)*, and ladle the jam into the jars to within ¼-inch of the tops.

5. Apply the lids and rings, and process in a hot water bath for 10 minutes *(see page 24)*.

SWEET WHITE WINE HONEY MUSTARD

YIELDS ABOUT 2 HALF-PINT JARS

s a rule of thumb, the colder the liquid you soak mus-
ard seeds in, the hotter the finished mustard will be.
o achieve a mild, mostly yellow, honey mustard, I use
om temperature wine to soak the mustard seeds. It
so mellows at room temperature before heading into
e refrigerator for long-term storage.

NGREDIENTS

cup yellow mustard seeds
cup brown mustard seeds
cup white wine*
tablespoons apple cider vinegar
cup honey
½ teaspoons Kosher salt, more to taste

- Combine the mustard seeds in a glass bowl and
  cover them with the white wine. Cover the bowl
  and let it sit at room temperature until the seeds
  have soaked up all of the wine (at least 4 hours).

- Sterilize the jars *(see page 22, step 2)*.

- Transfer the soaked mustard seeds to a food processor or blender, and add the remaining ingredients.

4. Process or blend (taking care not to puree the seeds completely), until the mustard has a creamy, homogenized look. Transfer the mustard into sterilized glass jars (they don't need to be packed all the way up to the top). Cover with the lids and rings, and let them sit at room temperature for 2 days before transferring to the refrigerator. The natural keeping power of the mustard will preserve it for at least up to 1 year.

Choose a wine that you prefer. A pinot grigio, vinho verde, or riesling are good options.

Note: The flavor of the mustard continues to change as it sits for the first few days, so you may wish to add more salt or honey after it rests.